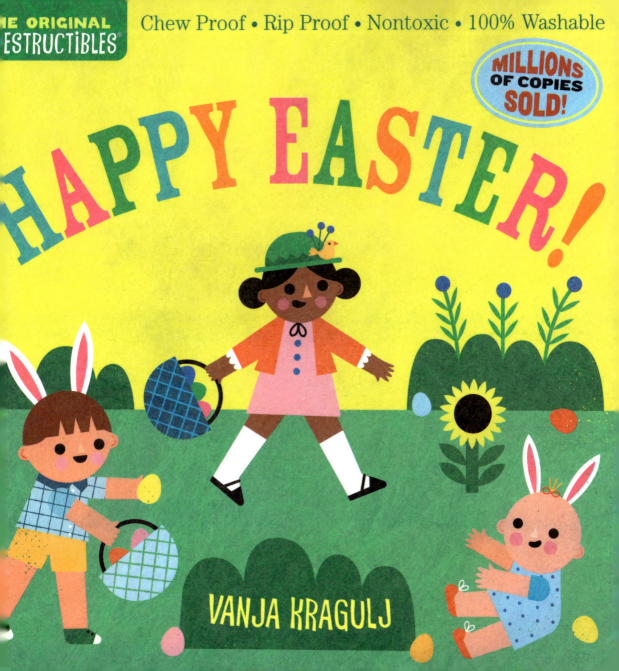

The Easter Bunny brought yummy treats!

Let's dye eggs and hide them in the garden!

dressed in their Easter best.

THE ORIGINAL INDESTRUCTIBLES®

For ages 0 and u[p]

BOOKS BABIES CAN REALLY SINK THEIR GUMS INTO!

It's Easter! Did the Easter Bunny bring something yummy?
Time for an Easter egg hunt. How many can you find?
Here comes the family. Happy Easter, everyone!

Share cherished holiday traditions with baby in a book that's INDESTRUCTIBL[E]

Dear Parents: INDESTRUCTIBLES are built for the way babies "read": with their hands and mouths. INDESTRUCTIBLES won't rip or tear and are 100% washable. They're made for baby to hold, grab, chew, pull, and bend.

← CHEW ALL THESE AND MO[RE]

$5.99 US / $8.99 Can.
ISBN 978-1-5235-1413-7

9 781523 514137   5059

Copyright © 2023 by Indestructibles, LLC. Used under license.
Illustrations copyright © 2023 by Vanja Kragulj.
All rights reserved.
Library of Congress Cataloging-in-Publication Data is available.
WORKMAN is a registered trademark of Workman Publishing Co., Inc.,
a subsidiary of Hachette Book Group, Inc.
First printing January 2023 | 10 9 8 7 6 5 4 3 2 1

All INDESTRUCTIBLES books have been safety-tested and me[et or]
exceed ASTM-F963 and CPSIA guide[lines.]
INDESTRUCTIBLES is a registered trademark of Indestructibles, [LLC.]
Contact specialmarkets@hbgusa.com regar[ding]
special discounts for bulk purcha[ses.]
Printed in C[hina]

WORKMAN PUBLISHING CO., INC. 1290 Avenue of the Americas, New York, NY 10104 • indestructiblesinc.com